EMOTIONAL MASTERY SERIES

DRAW COLOR & WRITE

Emo Masters™

SELINA JOY JACKSON, MA

This book was created by Selina Joy Jackson, MA

Special Thanks to:

Jackie Hernandez - Grahic Artist, who created all of the EMOMASTERS characters and Business Coach Trina for taking them to the next level. You ROCK!

All of the teachers and students who allowed me to teach and expand you. I appreciate you.

(c) Copright 2005-2024 EMOMASTERS
All Rights Reserved

ISBN (Paperback):   979-8-9914993-7-8
    (eBook):   979-8-9914993-8-5

Suicide and Crises Hotline: Call 988 for support 24/7.

Objectives of this Color, Draw, and Write Book

This easy to read and apply book is designed to:

• Empower you to handle your emotions more effectively and with EASE.
• Increase your self-awareness.
• Boost your self-regulation.
• Build resilience.
• Help you develop powerful self-esteem and unstoppable confidence.

If you wanted to master your emotions, why would that be important to you personally? List 3 reasons:

_____

_____

_____

This FUN book can help you do it with ease. Is that okay with you? Let's go!

DISCLAIMER - This publication contains the ideas and opinions of its author. It is intended to provide helpful and informative material on the subject matter covered. It is sold with the understanding that the author and publisher are not engaged in rendering professional services in the book. If the reader requires personal assistance or advice, a competent professional should be consulted. The author and publisher specifically disclaim any responsibility for any liability, loss, or risk, personal or otherwise, which is incurred as a consequence, directly or indirectly, of the use and application of any of the contents of this book.

© Copyright 2005-2024 EMOMASTERS™ All Rights Reserved

In Your Experience: Which one do you feel you're most like or that you want to be most like and why?

I'm most like or I'd like to be most like

_____

because_____

_____

_____

_____

Are You a MASTER of Your Emotions?

Directions: Mark each item as true or false.

		True	False
1	You stay out of trouble.		
2	You handle your emotions in a healthy way.		
3	You are friendly and never start conflicts with others.		
4	You know trusted people you can talk to about almost anything.		
5	When you feel angry, you usually remain calm.		
6	You know how to have fun safely.		
7	You do your best in school.		
8	In school, you enjoy yourself almost every day.		
9	You get along well with your teacher and your classmates.		
10	When you feel down, you can get yourself to feel better.		
	How many "true" answers do you have?		

YAY, FOR YOU!

If you checked six or more items as true, you're on your way to being a master of your emotions and your life. The ideas in this book will help you get there.

If you checked five or fewer items as true, you already know things could be better. The ideas in this book are even more valuable to you.

Three basic parts of becoming the master of your emotions are:

- ✓ you know better responses come with education.
- ✓ you're observing what other people do so you can learn from them.
- ✓ you do things now that will pay off later.

> observe = to watch carefully and learn from what you see

A healthy emotional life

- What is a healthy emotional life? Does it mean you're feeling up 100% of the time? Who is in charge of what you feel?

Understanding Communication Styles

Everyone communicates in their own way, and there are three main styles that people use: Visual, Auditory, and Kinesthetic. Understanding these styles can help you connect better with others.

1. Visual: Visual communicators like to "see" things. They use words like "look," "see," and "picture." They might say, "I see what you mean" or "Let's look at this." They understand best when they can see pictures, diagrams, or written words.

2. Auditory: Auditory communicators focus on "hearing" and "talking." They use words like "listen," "say," and "discuss." They might say, "I hear you" or "Let's talk about it." They understand best when they can hear information or talk things through.

3. Kinesthetic: Kinesthetic communicators feel things physically. They use words like "feel," "grasp," and "touch." They might say, "I feel this is right" or "Let's get a grip on this." They understand best when they can move, touch, or experience things physically.

Knowing these styles helps you understand how you and others prefer to communicate. When you match your words to the other person's style, you can communicate more clearly and avoid misunderstandings.

Which of these Communication Styles is MOST like you?

Visual	Auditory	Kinesthetic
Uses words like: see, show, look	Uses words like: talk, say, listen	Uses words like: feel, touch , cool
You enjoy eye-contact.	You like the sound of your own voice.	You enjoy hands-on stuff.

What kind of clues show how you're feeling?

Your facial expressions show how you feel.	Your tone of voice tells how you're feeling.	Your body language and movement gives clues about how your'e feeling

Understanding Communication Styles Quiz

1. What word might a Visual communicator use?
   a) Hear
   b) See
   c) Touch
   d) Feel

2. Which word would an Auditory communicator most likely use?
   a) Look
   b) Picture
   c) Discuss
   d) Grasp

3. What is a key word a Kinesthetic communicator might say
   a) Listen
   b) Look
   c) Feel
   d) See

4. How does a Visual communicator best understand information?
   a) By hearing it
   b) By seeing it
   c) By feeling it
   d) By touching it

5. If someone says, "Let's talk about it," which communication style are they using?
   a) Visual
   b) Auditory
   c) Kinesthetic
   d) All of the above

Answers are on the next page..

Calm Knight and the Mystery of Miscommunication

Calm Knight was a superhero known for his incredible ability to bring clarity, reassurance, and focus to any situation. His message, "Clear mind, calm heart, strong focus," guided him through countless challenges, helping others find peace and understanding in the most confusing of circumstances. But even Calm Knight wasn't immune to the difficulties of communication, especially when it came to understanding how people really felt.

One day, Calm Knight noticed that something was off among his closest friends. They had been working together on a mission, but lately, there seemed to be tension and misunderstanding between them. Conversations that used to flow easily now felt awkward, and there were moments of frustration that Calm Knight couldn't quite understand.

Determined to restore harmony among his friends, Calm Knight decided to investigate. He knew that people often say things but mean something else entirely because meaning is in people, not in words. To get to the bottom of the issue, Calm Knight decided to ask each of his friends a simple yet powerful question: "How do you know when you are respected?"

He began with his friend Valor, a brave and bold hero who always spoke his mind. "Valor," Calm Knight asked, "how do you know when someone respects you?"

Valor thought for a moment, then replied, "It's in the way people talk to me. I can hear it in the tone of their voice, the kinds of words they use. When someone respects me, they speak to me with care and consideration. They tell me that they respect me, and they don't argue with me just for the sake of it. Respect, to me, is all about what I hear."

Calm Knight nodded, understanding that for Valor, respect was communicated through words and tone—a very auditory way of perceiving the world.

Next, Calm Knight visited his friend Luminous, a hero known for her keen observational skills. "Luminous," he asked, "how do you know when someone respects you?"

Luminous smiled and said, "I see it in the way they look at me. When someone respects me, they give me their full attention, making eye contact when I speak. They show me that they're really listening and that they value what I have to say. They also notice beautiful things about me and acknowledge them. Respect, for me, is something I see."

Again, Calm Knight nodded, realizing that Luminous understood respect through visual cues—what she saw in others' behavior and their acknowledgment of her.

Finally, Calm Knight turned to his friend Serenity, a hero known for her gentle nature and nurturing spirit. "Serenity," he asked, "how do you know when someone respects you?"

Serenity took a deep breath and replied, "I feel it in the way they treat me. When someone respects me, they're gentle in their touch and thoughtful in their actions. They do things to make my life better and show care in the little things they do. Respect, to me, is all about how someone makes me feel."

Calm Knight nodded once more, understanding that Serenity experienced respect through touch and actions—a kinesthetic way of perceiving the world.

As Calm Knight reflected on these different answers, he realized that each of his friends had their own unique way of understanding respect—auditory, visual, and kinesthetic. The tension between them likely arose because they were communicating in ways that didn't align with each other's filters.

That evening, Calm Knight gathered his friends together. "I think I've found the root of our misunderstanding," he said calmly. "We all perceive respect in different ways. Valor, you hear it in words; Luminous, you see it in actions; and Serenity, you feel it through touch and care. But when we don't understand each other's ways of feeling respected, it can create disharmony."

His friends listened closely as Calm Knight continued. "What if we tried to express our respect in ways that match each other's preferences? Valor, we can make sure to speak with care and affirmation when talking to you. Luminous, we can give you our full attention and acknowledge what we see in you. And Serenity, we can show our respect through thoughtful actions and gentle gestures."

The room was filled with a sense of clarity and relief as the friends realized the simple yet profound truth that Calm Knight had uncovered. Miscommunication often happened not because they didn't respect each other, but because they were expressing it in different ways.

With this newfound understanding, the tension between them melted away. Calm Knight felt his own strength grow even deeper, knowing that he had helped his friends reconnect with each other through clarity, reassurance, and focus.

From that day forward, Calm Knight and his friends communicated more openly and effectively, always remembering to consider each other's unique perspectives. They had learned that true harmony came not just from speaking, but from understanding the meaning behind the words, the looks, and the gestures.

And so, Calm Knight continued his mission, always ready to bring clarity to confusion, calm to chaos, and focus to the most challenging of situations. He knew that with a clear mind, a calm heart, and a strong focus, anything was possible.

Story written by Selina Jackson with assistance from AI.

Which character traits would be most useful to you right now and why?

Draw or write your thoughts about.

Are You an Introvert or an Extrovert?

Here's a simple chart to help you figure out if you're more of an introvert or an extrovert. Check out the descriptions below and see which sounds most like you!

Extroverts	Introverts
Get energy from being with others	Get energy from being alone
Love talking and sharing ideas	Prefer thinking quietly first
Enjoy hanging out with friends	Enjoy quiet time by yourself
Feel bored when things are too quiet	Feel calm when things are quiet
Talk while thinking	Think before speaking
Like exciting, new activities	Like calm, familiar activities
Feel excited in busy places	Feel relaxed in peaceful places
Like to be the center of attention	Prefer to watch and listen

What did you find?

- If most of your answers match the Extroverts side, you might be an extrovert! You love being around people and sharing your thoughts and ideas. You get energized by hanging out with friends and trying new things.

- If most of your answers match the Introverts side, you might be an introvert! You enjoy your own company and need quiet time to recharge. You think before you speak and like calm, peaceful activities.

- If your answers are kind of equal between both, then you're both. Sometimes you need to be with people and sometimes it's best for you to be by yourself. You can also be with people but simply be quiet and to yourself.

Remember:
There's no right or wrong way to be. Whether you're an introvert, an extrovert, or a mix of both, what matters most is understanding yourself and how you feel best.

Mindful Doodling: Steps for You

1. Breathe In and Out:
- Before you start, take a deep breath in through your nose, hold it, and slowly breathe out through your mouth. Do this a few times to help you relax.

2. Draw a Shape:
- In the middle of your paper, draw a simple shape like a circle, square, or triangle.

3. Add Patterns:
- Around your shape, start drawing a pattern, like zigzags, waves, or spirals. Keep it simple and repeat the pattern.

4. Keep Going:
- Continue your pattern, slowly filling up the page with more lines and shapes. Take your time and focus on each line you draw.

5. Color (Optional):
- If you like, add some colors to your doodle. Choose colors that make you feel happy and calm.

6. Look at Your Drawing:
- When you finish, look at your drawing. How do you feel now? Notice if you feel more relaxed or happy.

7. Show and Share:
- If you want, show your drawing to someone and tell them about your patterns and colors.

Mindful Doodling Example:

I feel proud and relaxed after doing this.

Feel free to color this sheet and feel good.

MEET MOTION

Our superhero flows like emotions and has the power to control their emotions just like you.

DRAW MOTION!

Use the grid to finish the drawing.

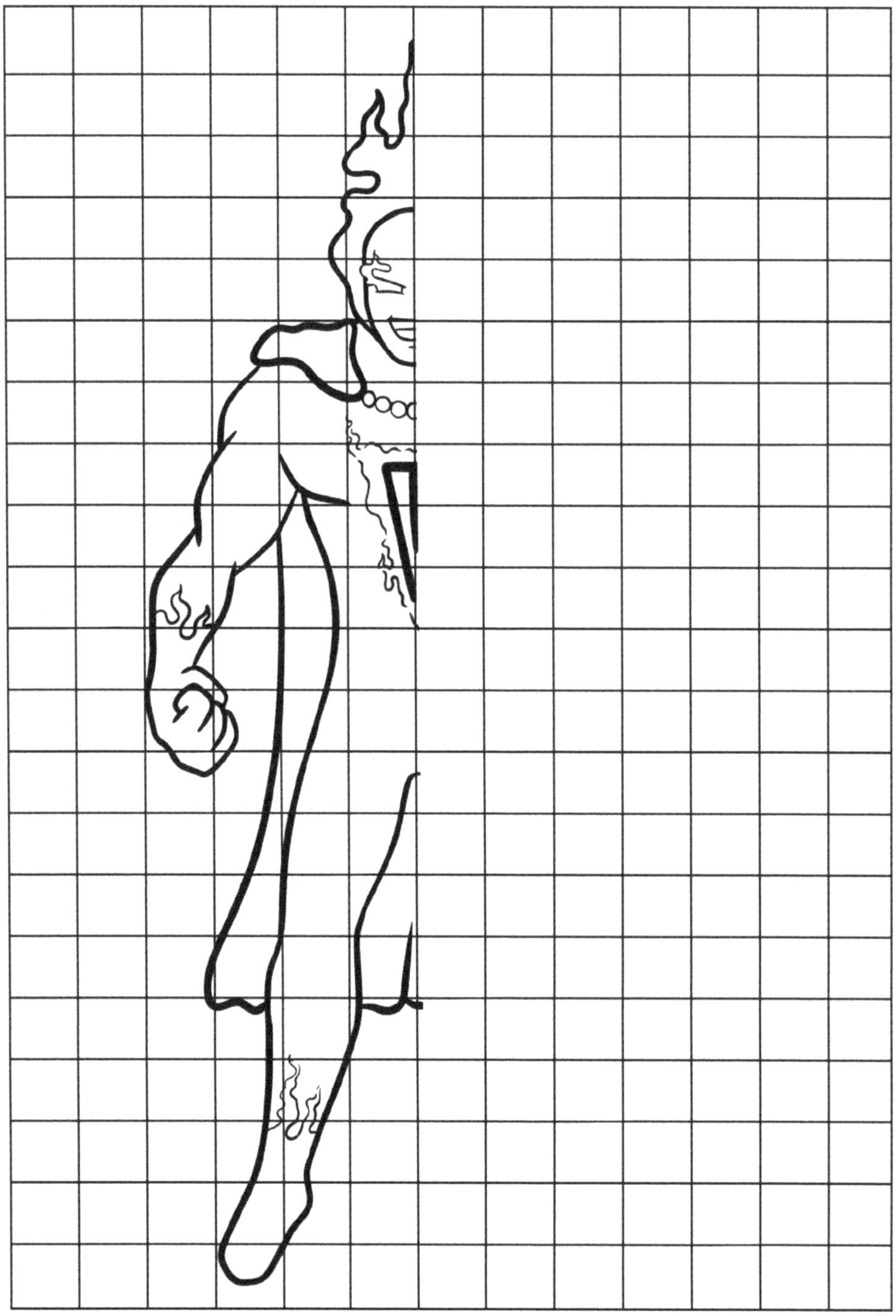

DRAW MOTION

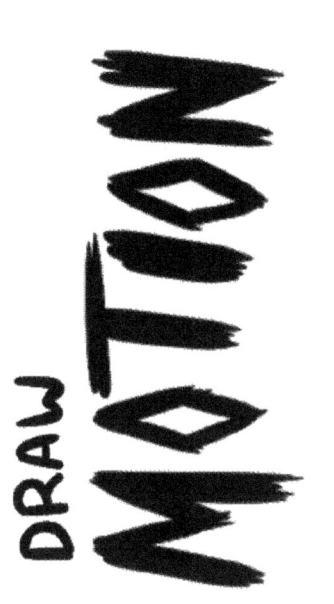

Use the grid to draw Motion!

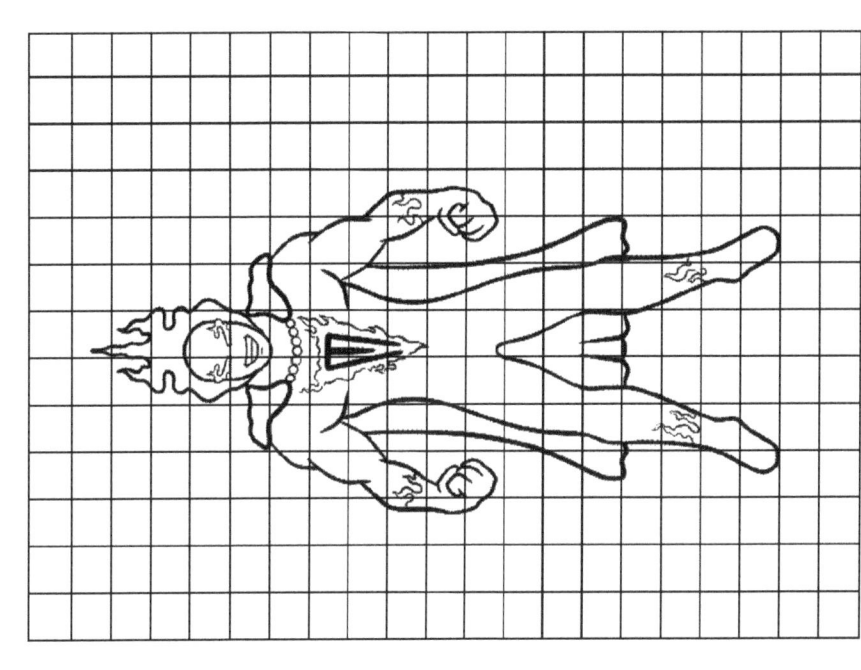

Which TLC (Thinking, Learning, and Communication) Style is most like you?

VAK Systems Behavioral Chart

	KINESTHETIC	AUDITORY	VISUAL
Learn best by:	doing it, hands-on experiences,	hearing, lectures, discussions	seeing, looking at demonstrations
If inactive or bored:	will move, put their hands on something	will talk aloud to self or to others, drum on table	stares at something; draw or doodle
Recalls best:	what was done	what they hear or say	what they see
Enjoys/needs:	action, movement, wiggling, space	music, debates, likes to talk	movies, reading, staring into space, doodling
Makes it hard for them to focus:	unfinished tasks, movement, having to sit still for long periods	sounds, noise	when things look messy
When feeling stressed or pressured:	finds it hard to be still	finds it hard to be quiet	finds it hard to talk or take action
How they approach problems or tasks:	avoids planning, jumps right in, then thinks about it later	needs to talk it out	likes to plan and organize, check off lists

What are your SUPER strengths?

Check all that are true for you.

__Bravery
__Fun personality
__Gratitude
__Honesty
__Perseverance (Keep going)
__I have people smarts
__I love learning

__Creativity
__Self-regulation (I control what I do, say, and feel)
__Hope
__Kindness
__Love
__Curious

__Other (List it here)_____

What are three struggles you want to OVERCOME this year?

List them here:

1.

2.

3.

Which of your strengths can you activate to overcome these struggles?

Understanding Your Emotions so You Can Master Them

Whether we know it or not, we are **always** feeling. If you're not aware of what you're feeling, that will create some MAJOR problems. And you'll painfully find yourself in deep doo-doo.

This section can help prevent and correct problems. Are you ready to learn something new and useful? Move forward.

Which character traits would be most useful to you right now and why?

Draw or write about it here.

LET'S FACE IT...
LIFE ISN'T FAIR

Things happen that you can't control.

Your SUCCESS depends on how well you handle those challenges.

WHAT CAN EMPOWER YOU?

Think of something that made you feel not so good.

Write what you were thinking in the thought bubble.

EXAMPLES:

*"I lost my phone.
I'm such an idiot."
"I just hate myself."
"I can't stand losing anything."*

How would you like to feel instead?

What are some thoughts that could make you feel that way? Write your answers in the thought bubble.

EXAMPLES:

"I am proud of myself for handling my anger well.
"I don't like losing my phone but I can handle it."
"It's okay to make mistakes. It means I'm learning and growing."

What if you knew that feeling better is just a thought away?

HOW TO HAVE MORE CONTROL OVER WHAT HAPPENS TO YOU

AN EVENT HAPPENS...

When you see things in a negative way, you will feel worse.

Seeing things in a positive way can lead to positive outcomes.

The meaning you give to an event makes you feel how you feel and do what you do.

You can decide how to feel about the things that happen to you.

Pulse and the Power of Restoration

Pulse, the superhero of restoration, was known across the city for his incredible ability to revive hope and restore strength in others. Whenever disaster struck or someone lost their way, Pulse was there to lift them up, reignite their spirit, and help them find their strength. But even a hero like Pulse had challenges of his own.

One sunny afternoon, Pulse returned to his neighborhood after a long day of helping others. As he approached his house, he noticed something strange—his neighbor, Mr. Griggs, was shouting angrily at a group of kids who had accidentally kicked a soccer ball into his yard. Pulse watched as Mr. Griggs grabbed the ball and refused to give it back, leaving the kids upset and on the verge of tears.

Pulse's first instinct was to rush over and restore peace, but something stopped him. He felt a surge of frustration bubbling up inside him. "Why does Mr. Griggs always have to be so mean?" Pulse thought. "I'm tired of dealing with his grumpiness every day."

As he walked inside, Pulse couldn't shake the negative thoughts swirling in his mind. He found himself sinking into the couch, feeling drained of energy. For a moment, Pulse forgot about his superpower—he forgot about the strength that lay within him.

Suddenly, a soft, glowing light appeared in front of him, filling the room with warmth. Pulse recognized it immediately—it was the Spirit of Restoration, a magical presence that had guided him many times before. The light began to swirl around him, and Pulse felt a familiar surge of energy returning to his body.

"Pulse," the Spirit whispered, "even you, the superhero of restoration, can be zapped of your strength when you hold on to negative thoughts. Remember, it's not the event that drains you, but the way you think about it."

The Spirit's words echoed in Pulse's mind, and he realized the truth. It wasn't Mr. Griggs' actions that made him feel powerless—it was his own thoughts about the situation. Pulse closed his eyes and began to ask himself some important questions:

"What am I feeling right now?"

He recognized the frustration and anger that had taken hold of him.

"What thoughts or images came into my mind right before I felt this way?"

He saw a picture of Mr. Griggs yelling at the kids and felt the unfairness of it all.

"How do I want to feel instead?"

Pulse envisioned himself feeling calm, strong, and in control of his emotions, just like he did when he helped others.

"What are some better thoughts that can get me to that feeling?"

He thought, "Mr. Griggs might be having a bad day, just like anyone else. Maybe he needs some help, too. I don't need to control his actions, but I can control how I respond."

As these new thoughts settled in, Pulse felt his energy return. He stood up, filled with the strength of restoration once more. He knew what he had to do.

Pulse walked over to Mr. Griggs' house and knocked on the door. When Mr. Griggs opened it, Pulse greeted him with a warm smile. "Hey, Mr. Griggs, I noticed you seemed upset earlier. Is everything okay?"

Mr. Griggs sighed and leaned against the doorframe. "It's just been one of those days, Pulse. Everything's going wrong, and I took it out on those kids. I shouldn't have done that."

Pulse nodded, understanding. "We all have days like that. But I've found that when I focus on what I can control, and let go of what I can't, things get better. How about we return the ball to the kids together and show them how we can make things right?"

Mr. Griggs looked surprised, but then he smiled—a rare sight for him. "You know, Pulse, that sounds like a good idea."

Together, they walked over to the kids, who were still waiting anxiously on the sidewalk. Mr. Griggs handed the ball back and apologized, and the kids' faces lit up with joy.

As Pulse watched the scene unfold, he felt the power of restoration wash over him. He had learned an important lesson that day: even when things seem out of control, he could choose how to think and feel about the situation. By changing his thoughts, he restored not only his own strength but also the peace and harmony of his neighborhood.

And so, Pulse continued his mission, stronger and wiser than before, always ready to revive hope, restore strength, and remind others—and himself—that true power comes from within.

This story was written by Selina Joy Jackson (with the assistance of chatgpt).

Which character traits would be most useful to you right now and why?

Draw or write about it here.

THE MESSAGE BEHIND THE FEELING

EMOTIONS ARE LIKE SECRET MESSAGES.

WHEN YOU UNDERSTAND WHAT EACH EMOTION MEANS, YOU CAN MAKE THE EMOTION GO AWAY.

NOT KNOWING CREATES PROBLEMS SUCH AS
MISTAKING FRUSTRATION FOR ANGER.

MAKE SURE YOU KNOW THE DIFFERENCE.
BE VERY CLEAR ABOUT WHAT EACH ONE MEANS.

MEANINGS OF EMOTIONS

"OKAY, POP QUIZ."

ANGER – SOMEONE HAS CROSSED YOUR BOUNDARIES OR DISHONORED YOUR VALUES.

FEAR – YOU THINK YOU'RE IN DANGER.

FRUSTRATION – YOU'RE TRYING TO GET SOMETHING AND SOMETHING IS IN THE WAY.

SADNESS – YOU THINK YOU'VE LOST SOMETHING.

THE EMOTIONS THAT CAUSE THE MOST TROUBLE ARE: FEAR, ANGER, AND SADNESS.

Often, people try to ignore or minimize these intense emotions because they feel like forever.

It's a mistake to ignore uncomfortable feelings. It puts you in conflict with yourself. And that triggers anxiety. So, now you have what I like to call a cocktail of emotions. If you don't solve that, it will affect all the other areas of your life. PAIN!

BETTER WAYS TO RESPOND TO UNCOMFORTABLE FEELINGS

1) Allow yourself to become aware of what you're feeling. Ask, *"what am I feeling right now?"*

2) Welcome it. Say, *"I welcome all of my feelings and all the reasons for them being here now."*
   I know it seems counterintuitive to do this but unless you do, it will keep knocking on your door until the door falls off the hinges.

3) Give yourself permission to feel it. Say, "It's okay for me to feel what I'm feeling.

   Now, you're ready to apply a soothing technique. Go to the next page.

HOW TO HANDLE ANGER

ASK YOURSELF:

WHO HAS CROSSED MY BOUNDARIES?

THEN, BE ASSERTIVE. THAT MEANS YOU:
    1) TELL THEM HOW YOU FEEL.
    2) ASK FOR WHAT YOU WANT.

Ok, here are the rules:

The Last Man Standing...

Goes To <u>Prison</u> !

DRAW some better ways to handle anger:

HOW TO HANDLE FEAR

FEAR: MAKE SURE THERE IS NO REAL DANGER.

IS THERE REALLY A FIRE BREATHING DRAGON UNDER MY BED?

UH...MY HAIR.

IF NOT, THAT MEANS YOUR BRAIN HAS CREATED A "FALSE DANGER SIGNAL."

TIME TO GET RID OF IT.

LET'S GO!

NEUTRALIZE THE FALSE MESSAGE

THE KEY IS TO APPLY TRUE SELF-LOVE.

HOW TO APPLY TRUE-SELF LOVE

WHEN YOU USE THE SCRIPT BELOW, IT NEUTRALIZES THE POWER OF THE SELF-HATRED.

It's Okay to Talk

When you're going through tough times, it's okay to talk with a counselor, your parents, or some healthy, mature adult who can help with trusted support.

A **challenge** for you: Memorize this and EMPOWER Yourself to feel happier and more FREE! (No matter what happens.

YOU
An Empowerment Chant

Verse 1:
Stuff happens, life's got twists and turns,
But how you see it, that's where the fire burns,
When something goes down, you got a choice to make,
See it in a bad light, man, that's a mistake.
You'll feel the weight, it's heavy on your chest,
But flip the script, start seeing it as a test.
When you view it right, the load feels light,
Turn it around, let the future shine bright.

Chorus:
You got the power, take control,
What you see is what you'll hold.
See it bad, feel the pain,
But see it good and watch the gain.
Change your mind, change your game,
How you feel is in your name.
Don't let the world tell you how to be,
Decide for yourself and set yourself free.

Verse 2:
It's not about what happens, it's about what you think,
Your thoughts shape your feelings, like ink to a link.
See the rain, you could moan or dance,
Take that chance, make life's stance.
When you give meaning, you give power too,
So why not choose the view that's true?
Feel the vibes, the energy you make,
It's in your hands, for your own sake.

Chorus:
You got the power, take control,
What you see is what you'll hold.
See it bad, feel the pain,
But see it good and watch the gain.
Change your mind, change your game,
How you feel is in your name.
Don't let the world tell you how to be,
Decide for yourself and set yourself free.

Chant by Selina Jackson with assistance from chatGPT.

Which character traits would be most useful to you right now and why?

Draw or write about it here.

RELEASE THE NEGATIVE EMOTION

DID YOU KNOW?

Your mind loves the word, 'release.' Anytime you say, I release something, it releases it instantly. Unless for some reason it doesn't want to; in which case you won't be able to make the statement or you'll make it with mistakes. In that case, back up and get rid of the unwillingness to release it it. Are you ready to free yourself?

RELEASE SCRIPT

1) Rate it. 0-10 (ten being strongest), how strong is the emotion?

2) Release it - SCRIPT:
- 'I release this _____.
- I release all the reasons for it.
- I release all the results of it.

RE-RATE IT:

3) RE-Rate It - 0-10, how strong is the fear now?
- If it is more than 2, release the unwillingness to let it go.

Re-rate it.
- Choose to replace the fear with love and trust.

WHAT IF YOU CHOOSE TO RECOGNIZE THE IMPORTANCE OF LETTING GO OF EMOTIONS TO ACHIEVE EMOTIONAL MASTERY?

Others have successfully use this powerful technique to get rid of:

- Anger (After releasing it, replace it with forgiveness).
- Anxiety
- All non-love (Then, choose to replace it with love).
- Sadness (after releasing, then ask yourself what's most important to you about the lost loved one or item? Then choose to recognize the importance of that person or phing.

MAKE A LIST OF TROUBLESOME EMOTIONS THAT YOU CAN USE THIS STRATEGY TO OVERCOME THEM WITH EASE.

Letting Go

List some feelings, or thoughts inside the balloons that you've decided to release so you can move forward successfully and with ease from now on.

EMPOWERING YOURSELF

IF YOU COULD DO ANYTHING BETTER IN HANDLING YOUR EMOTIONS THIS MONTH, WHAT WOULD IT BE?

WHAT IS THE FIRST THING YOU CAN DO TO MAKE THAT HAPPEN?

SHARING YOUR GRATITUDE IS AN EASY, POWERFUL WAY TO FEEL HAPPIER.

DID YOU KNOW YOU CAN OVERCOME NEGATIVE EMOTIONAL EPISODES EASIER WHEN...

I'M LOOKING AT HOW FLY MY HAIR LOOKS!

Look for the good!

EVERYTHING IS RELATIONSHIPS

Are you on your own side? Do you have your own back? Do you really accept yourself no matter what? The way you secretly feel about yourself is how others will treat you.

If you hate the way you feel, you'll keep attracting situations that allow you to experience more hate. Fortunately, choosing to love and accept yourself no matter what will change the trajectory of the magnet.

THE MORE YOU IMPROVE YOUR RELATIONSHIP WITH YOUR EMOTIONS, THE BETTER YOUR RELATIONSHIPS OF ALL KINDS.

SUPER BOOST YOUR RESULTS

PICK AN IDEA FROM THIS CHAPTER. DRAW A CARTOON ABOUT THAT IDEA.

WHAT DOES EACH EMOTION MEAN?

OBVIOUSLY, YOU WANT TO:

HOW DO YOU SEE YOURSELF USING THESE UNCOMMON TOOLS TO DO IT WITH EASE AND CERTAINTY FROM NOW ON?

CONGRATULATIONS!

Are You A Good Listener?

What is it like when someone is in a good listening mood? Indicate the behaviors that accurately describe good listening.

Behavior	Yes	No
Asking questions to clarify what you heard		
Looking around the room rather than at the speaker		
Paraphrasing what the speaker said to make sure you understand		
Talking to someone else while the speaker is talking		
Listening to the speaker's tone of voice		
Noticing how the speaker is breathing (fast/shallow, or slow and deep)		
Giving unsolicited advice		
Changing the subject before the speaker is finished		
Watching the speaker's body language to get greater meaning		
List the top three behaviors you believe comprise good communication:		
1.		
2.		
3.		

Discussion:

One of the biggest barriers to good communication is when a person does not listen actively. Active listening is not just hearing the verbal, it is picking up on the person's non-verbal signals, as well; facial expressions, tone of voice, body language, etc.

In fact, the non-verbal cues people send comprise 83% of the message, while verbal carries a low 13%. If the words convey one meaning, while the body language conveys another, then these two message sending channels are out of sync.

Being able to decipher what a person is really saying is key to good communication. After all, good communication affects every area of your life. It is the essence of getting what we want easier. What will you do to increase your communication skills?

NEGATIVITY HACK: TAKE IT BACK!

Negativity Hacks	Example:	Counteract it with:
Negative Hack from the Past	I missed that shot in the game last week. That means I suck at basketball.	"I now choose to believe that my past doesn't determine my future. I make my future better."
Negative Hack from the Present	I don't like what they said about me.	Neutralize it with: "I cancel that"
Stop the Madness	What they said makes me feel bad.	Use this positive power filter: "I have decided to prevent others from making me feel bad."

Help our graphic artist, Jackie H. finish her picture. Trace the lines and draw in more of the picture.

Negativity Hack!

What are some negative thoughts you've had?

I CANCEL THAT!!

How to Feel More Powerful and Good about Yourself

Play the, "I Cancel That!" Game

Just like a magnet, we attract what we think, say, and feel. We talk to ourselves. We talk to ourselves at the rate of 500-1500 words a minute. Wow! Did you get that? That's a lot of words we hear in our heads. Psychologists call it *self-talk*. We do it so often; we don't even pay attention to whether what we are saying supports our success or sabotages it.

But there is a way to tell instantly if what we're saying to ourselves creates good energy or bad energy. Our feelings will let us know. If we feel positive, then our self-talk is working for and not against us. It's bringing our dreams, and goals, and desires closer.

If we feel negative, that's the signal that something is wrong. Our self-talk and feelings are pushing what we really want further away.

So, it is important to upgrade our minds to speak words of encouragement. When we are young and unable to take care of ourselves, others tell us what to do, what to say, how to think. Some of what we hear may not always be positive.

But now, your eyes are on this page, you are reading this right now. That means you are now old enough to cancel out any negative statements you may have heard, or have been saying to yourself and replace them with positive ones. Then, you get to feel stronger and good about yourself. Is that okay?

ACTION STEPS

1. Whenever you catch yourself thinking something negative, say "I cancel that." (you can even say it inside your head). And that will stop that thought from making you feel bad.
2. Then, choose to replace it with a power statement like the ones below.

> **Power Statements**
>
> - I give thanks.
> - What if I am twice as confident as a student from now on?
> - Every day, every way, I'm getting better and better. (say 2x's)
> - I allow myself to feel calm and happy with speed and ease.
> - I now choose to believe that I am capable and powerful. YES!

© Copyright 2009 Selina J. Jackson, M.A. All Rights Reserved

Move and Feel Better Faster

Did you know many people hold emotions in their bodies? It's true and one way to shake 'em off is to move.

Which character traits would be most useful to you right now and why?

Draw or write about it here.

Welcome to Happier Relationships!

Have you ever felt like understanding friends, family, or even yourself is like solving a puzzle? Well, guess what? You're not alone! In this section, you're going to explore fun activities that will help you feel happier, more confident, and free in all your relationships. Whether it's with friends, family, teachers, or even YOU, these exercises will teach you cool ways to communicate better, handle conflicts like a pro, and even discover your hidden strengths.

Think of it like a superhero training camp—but for your social life. Ready to power up and create awesome connections? Let's dive in and level up your relationship game!

Friendships are good.

What are you doing to make and keep GOOD friends?

List 3 important qualities in a good friend:

1.
2.
3.

Helping you to feel more powerful and good about yourself!

GAMEPLAYS - Tic-Tac-Toe Blackout Interview

Choose a family member, classmate, or friend. Ask them one of the questions and pay attention to their response. Then write their name in the box. Make sure you choose a different person for each box. This can help you strengthen your social connections. That is an asset for you.

If you chose a hashtag to describe your life right now, what would it be? Name: _____	If you were to create a national holiday, what would it be? Name: _____	What is one hidden talent or strength you have that you wish people knew about? Name: _____
Whom do you admire the most and why? Name: _____	What do you think is the biggest danger when it comes to kids using the internet? Name: _____	When things get difficult, what do you do to encourage yourself? Name: _____
If you started a band, what would you name it and why? Name: _____	What negative emotions do you sometimes feel when using social media platforms like Instagram, Tik-Tok, or _____? (Name one) Name: _____	Who makes you smile the most? Name: _____

What did you discover about yourself?

What did you discover about relationships?

63

Think of some affirmations to tell yourself:

Write them on the mirror.

I am smart.

I am intelligent.

Do What You Love

 You can spend time and money. You can replace the money, but you can never get back the time.

Use it wisely.

ARE YOU A STRESS MASTER? *(Test Your Skills)*

Take this little quiz and find out. Circle the number that describes your typical behavior.

1. I find ways to have fun and relaxation everyday.

    Never true   1   2   3   4   5   6   7   Always True

2. When facing difficulty, I look for what I can do to make the situation better.

    Never true   1   2   3   4   5   6   7   Always True

3. I do some form of exercise every day.

    Never True   1   2   3   4   5   6   7   Always True

4. I choose how I will respond in situations and more often than not, I respond in a positive way.

    Never true   1   2   3   4   5   6   7   Always True

5. I see humor everyday. I like to smile. I find reasons to laugh.

    Never true   1   2   3   4   5   6   7   Always True

6. I put myself into good moods whenever I choose.

    Never true   1   2   3   4   5   6   7   Always True

7. I use negotiation to get what I want.

    Never true   1   2   3   4   5   6   7   Always True

8. I make tracks instead of excuses and avoid blaming others for how I feel.

    Never true   1   2   3   4   5   6   7   Always True

9. I know how to and will make myself feel better whenever I want to, without. causing problems for myself.

    Never true   1   2   3   4   5   6   7   Always True

10. When someone does something that I don't like, I respond in ways that are respectful to myself and others.

    Never true   1   2   3   4   5   6   7   Always True

STRESS MASTER Score Sheet

Directions:
1. Add up your circled numbers.
2. Read the three scoring sections below.
3. Allow your subconscious mind to work out a personal meaning that works for you.

A score of"

60 and above suggests that you:
Realize that stuff happens. You can't control what is going on out there. In fact, it's the stuff that makes life happen. In addition, you see that since you can control what you think about the stuff, you can therefore control what you feel about the stuff, and that can very often swing the outcome to your favor. You are a stress master!
- You are good at getting what you want without needless hassle.
- You enjoy life.
- You'd prefer to laugh rather than grumble.
- You experience a high level of satisfaction.
- You feel positive, strong, and happy more often than not.

50-59 suggests that you:
Realize that as long as you live in this world, things will happen. You're making more and more improvements in your thinking, taking more control of your feelings, and therefore getting even better at mastering stress. Additional benefits include:
- You now realize that you have more control than you thought.
- People are starting to notice your efforts.
- With each passing moment, you feel more positive, strong, and happy.
- You're realizing more and more what you can do to get more satisfaction in your life.
- You're smiling now more than ever.

40-49 suggests that:
Don't realize that people don't feel the way they do because of something that happened; they feel the way they do because of what they THINK about what happened.

- You don't believe that you are strong and capable.
- You don't realize that your thinking makes or breaks your success.
- You don't realize just how much control you do have.
- You probably don't feel very good, laugh a whole lot, or get what you really want without unnecessary trouble.

I have one question for you:

*Are things **bad enough now** to make a change, or do you want to wait until they are **even worse**?*

SOLVING CONFLICTS

Solving conflicts is like solving a puzzle. You have to make sure you have the pieces that fit.

HOW TO USE THE 'QUESTIONING STRATEGY' TO GET RID OF STRESSFUL FEELINGS

Where do your feelings come from?	Ask POSITIVE Questions about Things and about Self
You can't have a feeling without words or picture. 90% of all thinking is in question form.	*What can I do today to feel more successful?* *Why is this working so well?* *Why am I enjoying this so much?*
Gaining a Deeper Understanding of Yourself so You Can Be Happier When you find yourself feeling bad, ask: *What was I saying or picturing in my mind that caused me to feel that?* The answer will come up. Now, it's time for you to decide whether you want those things to be true for you and real for you. Or, if you'd like to transform that into something better. The next questions can help do that: *What if I allow myself to think the kinds of thoughts that leave me feeling better about this situation?*	**In Your Experience** If you wanted to use the "Questioning Strategy' to feel better faster from now on, why would that be important to you personally? _____ If you can answer YES to these three questions, that means you are well on your way to feeling happier and more free: - Do you know how to use this strategy to get yourself to feel better? - Are you willing to use it from now on? - Will you use it from now on? Your eyes are on this page. You're reading this now. And that means you have every reason to expect that you'll notice more and more improvement in the way you handle your feelings and get yourself to feel better healthily. Is that okay with you?

Super Switch Technique

When you find yoursellf feeling down.:

1. Notice your thoughts. Most likely they are rehearsing the problem, something that you DON'T want. The problem with that is whatever you focus on you get more of.

2. Switch them from the problem to solution. Ask yourself:

    ☐ What is it that I want to happen (instead)?
    ☐ What needs to happen in order for that to happen?

3. Then, make a decision for that outcome. Focus on that.

Remember, what you focus on, the brain makes you do it.

Color and Consider: How can you use the Super Switch Technique to make completing homework easier?

Voices Behind the Conversation

Anytime you're having a conversation, there are actually HIDDEN voices influencing you. How can you make sure you're listening to the encouraging ones?

Write in some positive words in the speech bubbles to remind yourself to pay attention to the GOOD.

Five Steps to Unlock Your Creativity

One of the most powerful tools you can use to solve problems is your creativity. When you invite your creative side to help, you'll find solutions you never imagined before. Whether you're facing a challenging situation or feeling stuck, following these steps can help open the door to new ideas and possibilities.

Step 1: Ask the Magic Question
Start by asking yourself this: *"If I could push a button and solve this problem, how would I know it's solved?"* Imagine that the solution is already here. What would you be thinking? What actions would you be taking? What would you expect to happen next? This question helps your mind visualize the outcome and invites your creative side to begin exploring possibilities.

Step 2: Get Moving – Dance It Out!
Once you've asked the question, put on your favorite song and dance! Movement is a fun and powerful way to tap into your creativity. Dancing gets you out of your head and into your body, which can help loosen up stuck thoughts. As you dance, pay attention to any new ideas or thoughts that come to you. Sometimes, moving your body can unlock new pathways in your mind.

Step 3: Imagine Different Possibilities
Now that you're in a creative flow, take a few minutes to imagine different ways you could solve the problem. No idea is too wild or silly. Let your imagination run free! What are some unexpected solutions? What's something fun you could try that you haven't thought of before?

Step 4: Ask for Help
Creativity thrives when we collaborate with others. If you're feeling stuck, don't be afraid to ask someone for help. Sometimes a fresh perspective from a friend, family member, or mentor can spark a new idea. You can also ask your creative self for help—envision your creative part sitting beside you, ready to guide you toward the best solution.

Step 5: Take Action on Your Ideas
Now that you've opened up to your creativity, take action! Whether it's a small step or a bold move, doing something with your ideas brings you closer to solving the problem. Trust in your creative process and let each action guide you toward new insights.

By using these steps, you'll find that your creative side has more power than you think when it comes to solving problems. So next time you're facing a challenge, don't try to force the solution—invite your creativity to help instead!

Creative Self-Expression

Color and Consider: What ignites your creative expression?

Motion and the Power to Move Forward

In a city where the streets were filled with dreams waiting to be realized, there lived a hero known as Motion. His message was simple yet powerful: "Unleash Your Power - Move Forward." Motion was no ordinary hero—he wasn't just about speed or agility. He was the embodiment of inner wisdom, the spark that ignites when we're ready to break free from the chains that hold us back.

One day, as Motion moved through the city, he sensed something troubling. The once-bustling streets were quieter than usual, and the air felt heavy with the weight of unspoken fears. He followed his instincts to a small community center where he found a group of people gathered, their faces clouded with worry and doubt.

As Motion observed from a distance, he began to hear their thoughts, whispers of fears that held them captive:

"I'm afraid to start because what if I fail?"

"I'm scared of what will happen if I actually succeed."

"I don't want the responsibility that comes with success. What if I can't handle it?"

"I can't bear the thought of being judged. What if people see me fail?"

These were the hidden fears that plagued them, the shadows that kept them from moving forward. Motion knew that these fears were like anchors, holding them in place, preventing them from unleashing their true power.

Motion stepped into the room, though not in the usual heroic fashion. This time, he appeared as a soft breeze that rustled the curtains, as a gentle voice in their minds, a whisper that felt both familiar and comforting—like their own inner wisdom speaking to them.

One by one, Motion approached each person, guiding them through their fears.

First, he found Sarah, a young artist who was paralyzed by the fear of failure. She hadn't picked up her brushes in weeks, afraid that her next painting would fall short of her expectations. Motion sat beside her, invisible to the eye but clear in her mind.

"Sarah," Motion whispered, "your fear is like a storm cloud, but remember, storms pass. What's underneath is the clear sky of your potential. What's the worst that could happen if you fail? You'll learn, and you'll grow stronger."

As Sarah let the words sink in, she felt a weight lift off her chest. She picked up a brush and began to paint, her strokes bold and free. Motion's gentle encouragement had unleashed her power to move forward.

Next, Motion turned to Jake, a successful businessman who secretly feared the weight of his own success. "What if I can't keep up?" he often wondered. "What if I crumble under the pressure?"

Motion appeared as a comforting presence in Jake's mind. "Jake, your fear is like a mountain, but every mountain has a path. Success doesn't mean you carry the world on your shoulders. It means you've learned how to navigate, how to ask for help when you need it. Trust in your journey, and the mountain will not seem so high."

Jake felt a surge of confidence, realizing that he didn't have to carry the burden alone. He smiled, feeling lighter, and ready to face whatever challenges lay ahead.

Finally, Motion approached Emily, a young writer who was terrified of being judged. She had a notebook full of stories, but she couldn't bring herself to share them with the world. "What if people don't like what I write?" she thought. "What if they laugh at me?"

Motion's presence was a gentle nudge, a reminder of her own strength. "Emily," he whispered, "your fear is like a mask, hiding your true face. But masks are meant to be taken off. You don't write for the approval of others—you write because your words are your truth. Trust in that, and the fear will dissolve."

Emily took a deep breath, and with Motion's guidance, she opened her notebook and began to write. This time, she wrote not with fear, but with love and trust in her own voice.

As the people in the room began to overcome their fears, Motion smiled, feeling the energy shift from doubt to determination. He knew that each of them had faced their own inner storm, but with his help, they had found the calm within, the strength to move forward.

Motion's work was done for the day, but his message lingered in the air, like a melody that stays with you long after the song is over. "Unleash your power—move forward," he reminded them, as he quietly disappeared into the breeze.

The city seemed brighter, the streets more alive, as the people stepped out of the community center, ready to take on the world. They had faced their fears, thanks to Motion, and now they knew that those fears were not walls, but doors—doors that led to new possibilities.

And so, Motion continued his journey, always there when someone needed that gentle push to break free from the chains of fear. He was the inner wisdom that lived in everyone, the quiet voice that said, "You are enough. You are strong. And you have the power to move forward."

And with each step, each choice to embrace love and trust over fear, the people of the city found themselves closer to their true selves, ready to unleash their power and move forward into the life they were meant to live.

This story written by Selina Jackson with the assistance of chatGPT.

Which character traits would be most useful to you right now and why?

Draw or write about it here.

Preparing for a Bright, Happy, and Successful Future

Did you know that the future is already in your hands? It might not feel like it now, but the choices you make today can shape your tomorrow. While there are influencers all around—friends, family, and even social media—there's one influence that matters most: *you*. Your thoughts and secret feelings about yourself are more powerful than you realize, and they can guide your future success and happiness.

The activities in this section are designed to help you unlock that power. By focusing on the positive, you can change how you feel and how things turn out. So, take control and start planning for a future where you succeed in school, build amazing relationships, and achieve your dreams. After all, the best way to predict your future is to create it! Ready to take that next step? Let's go!

Imagine Having the BEST, Most Successful High School Experience...

In Your BEST Most Successful High School Experience

1. What do you see around you?

2. What do you hear?

3. What are you saying to yourself?

4. What are you doing?

5. How are you feeling?

What if you make up your mind to have this or something better? Is that okay with you?

Congratulations!

Sereni Star and the Power of True Harmony

Sereni Star, the superhero with the power to bring harmony to any situation, was known far and wide for her ability to create peace and balance. Her message, "Harmony in every heartbeat," was a beacon of hope to everyone she met. But even Sereni Star, with all her strength and wisdom, wasn't immune to the challenges of being a superhero—especially when it came to peer pressure.

One day, Sereni Star found herself at the Superhero Academy, where young heroes in training learned to harness their powers. She was there to mentor a group of new students, each with their own unique abilities. The Academy was a lively place, full of excitement and energy, but it was also a place where competition and egos could sometimes get in the way of harmony.

During a training session, Sereni Star noticed a group of older students gathering around the newcomers, teasing them for their inexperience. The new heroes in training looked nervous and unsure of themselves, their confidence fading with each mocking word. Sereni Star felt a twinge of discomfort. She knew this wasn't right, but when she saw the older students looking her way, she hesitated.

"Come on, Sereni," one of the older students called out, grinning. "It's all in good fun. Don't be such a softie!"

Sereni Star felt a pang of guilt. She didn't want to be seen as weak or different. She could feel the pressure building, urging her to join in, but deep down, she knew this wasn't who she was. Sereni Star was about harmony, not hurt. But in that moment, the fear of being judged by her peers began to cloud her judgment.

As the teasing continued, Sereni Star found herself withdrawing, losing touch with her true self. She felt trapped between her desire to fit in and her inner voice that screamed for her to do the right thing. The more she struggled with her feelings, the more out of harmony she became.

That night, Sereni Star couldn't sleep. She tossed and turned, replaying the events of the day in her mind. "Why didn't I stand up for those new students?" she thought, her heart heavy with guilt. "Why did I let myself get caught up in what others think?"

Then, something remarkable happened. As Sereni Star lay in bed, she felt a gentle warmth spreading through her chest—a soft, rhythmic pulse that reminded her of her own heartbeat. It was as if the harmony she brought to others was calling her back to herself.

In that moment of quiet reflection, Sereni Star asked herself some important questions:

"What am I feeling right now?" she wondered. She realized she felt guilty, not just for her actions, but for betraying her own values.

"What thoughts or images came into my mind right before I felt this way?" She saw herself worrying about what the older students thought, fearing that they wouldn't accept her if she didn't go along with them.

"How do I want to feel instead?" Sereni Star pictured herself standing tall, confident, and true to her message of harmony.

"What are some better thoughts that can get me to that feeling?" She thought, "True strength isn't about fitting in—it's about being true to myself. Harmony comes from within, and I can bring that to any situation."

With renewed clarity, Sereni Star knew what she had to do. She realized that as a superhero, she had two powerful options: she could either resist the crowd or lead the crowd. And in this case, she chose to lead.

The next day at the Academy, Sereni Star approached the group of older students. "I've been thinking about what happened yesterday," she said, her voice calm but firm. "Teasing the new heroes isn't what being a superhero is about. We're here to help each other grow, not tear each other down."

The older students looked surprised, but Sereni Star continued. "I know you all have great strengths. Why not use them to lift others up instead of pushing them down? We can create a stronger, more united team if we support each other."

For a moment, there was silence. Then, one of the older students nodded. "You're right, Sereni. We got carried away. That's not the kind of heroes we want to be."

With Sereni Star's leadership, the mood at the Academy changed. The older students apologized to the newcomers, and soon, everyone was working together as a team. The new heroes in training felt more confident, and Sereni Star knew she had made the right choice by staying true to herself.

Sereni Star had faced a tough challenge, but she emerged stronger and more in harmony with her true self. She had learned that impressing others and gaining respect wasn't about following the crowd—it was about leading with integrity and staying true to her values.

As Sereni Star watched the heroes in training practice together, she felt a deep sense of peace. She had taken control in a high-pressure situation, gained valuable knowledge, and demonstrated that true harmony begins with being true to yourself.

And with every heartbeat, Sereni Star knew that she was living her message: Harmony in every heartbeat.

What can you do to make the world a better place?

Write some words on this page to share your answer..

YOU ARE YOUR OWN SUPERHERO

Title: Unstoppable Me: Writing Your Own Empowering Lyrics

Introduction:
Welcome, young lyricists! Have you ever felt like you're facing a big challenge, whether at school or at home? Well, guess what? You're not alone! Sometimes, expressing how we feel through words can make us feel stronger and more confident. In this activity, we're going to write eight bars of lyrics or rhymes that describe how we're overcoming a struggle and feeling unstoppable! Are you ready to unleash your inner songwriter? Let's get started!

Step 1: Finding Your Inspiration
Think about a time when you faced a tough situation but found a way to overcome it. It could be a difficult math problem, a disagreement with a friend, or anything else that made you feel challenged. Remember how you felt when you conquered that obstacle – proud, strong, and confident!

Step 2: Brainstorming
Use the Grab a piece of paper or your journal and jot down some words or phrases that describe your experience. Think about how you felt before, during, and after overcoming the challenge. Use descriptive words that paint a picture of your journey to victory.

Step 3: Getting Creative
Now, let's turn those words and phrases into catchy lyrics or rhymes! You have eight bars to work with, so make each line count. You can rhyme if you want to, but it's not necessary – what's important is that your lyrics reflect your feelings of empowerment and confidence.

Step 4: Putting It All Together
Once you've crafted your lyrics, read them out loud to see how they flow. Make any adjustments necessary to ensure that your message comes across loud and clear. Feel free to add a catchy hook or chorus to make your song even more memorable!

Step 5: Sharing Your Masterpiece
Congratulations, you've written your own empowering lyrics! Now, it's time to share your creation with the world. Whether you perform it for your classmates, family, or friends, remember to sing it with confidence and pride. You are unstoppable!

GOOD NEWS! There are some easy and fun example Lyrics and rhymes on the next page.

© Copyright 2005-2024 EMOMASTERS™ Selina Jackson, MA All Rights Reserved

Example Lyrics:

(Verse 1)
I faced a challenge, felt so small,
But I stood tall, gave it my all.
With every step, I grew stronger,
Now I know I can't go wronger.

(Verse 2)
I found my voice, I found my power,
No obstacle can make me cower.
I'm brave, I'm bold, I'm unafraid,
I'll rise above, I won't be swayed.

(Chorus)
I'm unstoppable, I'm feeling free,
Nothing can hold me back, you'll see.
I'll face each challenge with a grin,
Because I know that I will win!

Rhyming words

Rhyme Time	
Sure, here's a list of rhyming words that you can use to write their lyrics: 1. Strong 2. Long 3. Song 4. Along 5. Wrong 6. Thrive 7. Strive 8. Alive 9. Drive 10. Dive 11. Pride These words can help you create engaging rhymes and express themselves creatively in their lyrics.	12. Guide 13. Side 14. Glide 15. Wide 16. Bright 17. Fight 18. Might 19. Height 20. Light 21. Right 22. Delight 23. Sight 24. Night 25. Flight 26. Tight 27. Insight 28. Excite 29. Knight 30. Unite

More Rhyming Words that you can use to write your lyrics: 1. Strong 2. Long 3. Brave 4. Wave 5. Pride 6. Guide 7. Tall 8. Call 9. Grin 10. Win 11. Power 12. Flower 13. Free 14. Key 15. Bright These words can help you add rhythm and flow to your lyrics while expressing your feelings of strength and confidence!	16. Fight 17. Rise 18. Prize 19. Bold 20. Cold 21. Stand 22. Land 23. Goal 24. Soul 25. Confident 26. Sent 27. Cheer 28. Near 29. Unstoppable 30. Able

Conclusion:

You did it! You wrote your own empowering lyrics that celebrate your strength, resilience, and unstoppable confidence. Remember, no matter what challenges come your way, you have the power to overcome them and achieve greatness. Keep believing in yourself and keep shining bright!

EmoTress and the Power of Assertiveness

EmoTress was known among her friends for her deep understanding of emotions. She could sense when someone was feeling down, anxious, or even joyful, and she always knew the right thing to say. But today, something strange happened that made her question everything she believed in.

It all started when her friend, Maya, began acting differently. Maya, usually cheerful and kind, suddenly seemed distant and angry. She snapped at EmoTress over little things, and worst of all, EmoTress overheard her talking behind her back to other friends. "EmoTress is always so sensitive," Maya had said. "Sometimes I think she just needs to toughen up."

Hurt and confused, EmoTress felt a surge of anger. How could Maya, her close friend, say such hurtful things? EmoTress felt like her voice didn't matter, like she was being ignored and disrespected. The anger inside her grew, and for the first time, she was tempted to lash out. She thought about saying something mean in return or ignoring Maya completely. But deep down, she knew that wouldn't solve anything.

Days passed, and the tension between them grew. EmoTress started avoiding Maya, but it didn't make her feel any better. Then, one evening, something mystical happened. As she was sitting alone, pondering the situation, a soft, warm glow surrounded her. The glow was comforting, like a gentle hug, and suddenly, she felt a deep sense of calm.

A voice, soft and kind, whispered in her ear: "To feel seen and heard, you must speak up. But remember, strength comes not from anger, but from assertiveness."

The words echoed in her mind. She knew what she had to do. The next day, she found Maya sitting alone and approached her, feeling a bit nervous but determined.

"Maya," she began softly, "I need to talk to you about something that's been bothering me. When you yelled at me and talked behind my back, it hurt me. I felt like my voice didn't matter, like you didn't respect me."

Maya looked up, surprised. "EmoTress, I had no idea you felt that way," she said, her voice full of regret. "I didn't mean to hurt you. I was just going through some tough stuff and took it out on you without thinking."

EmoTress felt a weight lift off her shoulders. "I understand, but I want us to respect each other's feelings. If something's bothering you, can we talk about it instead of hurting each other?"

Maya nodded, tears welling up in her eyes. "I'm so sorry, EmoTress. I promise to be more mindful, and I hope you can forgive me."

The two friends hugged, and EmoTress felt something powerful inside her—she felt seen, she felt heard, and most importantly, she felt strong.

From that day forward, EmoTress knew that true strength didn't come from staying silent or lashing out. It came from being assertive—speaking up about how you feel and asking for what you need. And with that knowledge, she continued to help others understand their emotions, always with kindness and the power of her voice.

Story by Selina Jackson with assistance from chatGPT

Are You Being a STRONG Leader (Modeling GOOD things)?

What are some examples of a strong leader?
1) Doing something kind and to make the school a better place.
2) Lifting people UP with your words (Not bringing them down)
3) Giving compliments
4) Encouraging yourself (Saying stuff like):
    - "That's good!"
    - "I did a good job."
    - "I refuse to be negative."
    - "What if I have released all self-doubt?"

Give some examples of each:

Weak Leadership	STRONG Leadership
1)	1)
2)	2)
3)	3)

GETTING STRONGER	How did it make you feel?
1) What did you do that was NOT strong leadership this week?	
2) What have you done this week that shows what a strong leader really is?	
3) What will you do today to become an even **stronger** leader?	

0-10, ten being most proud, how proud of yourself are you right now? _____

Now you know just how powerful you really are!

From now on, whenever something happens that you don't like, you will respond in ways that are respectful to yourself and others.

Name two ways:
1. _____
2. _____

Remember: How you think about things will change how you feel, which will impact your response.

What if you choose to interpret things in a more positive way?

So you can be HAPPIER AND MORE FREE NO MATTER WHAT

COPYRIGHT 2013-2022 EMOMASTERS™ Selina Joy Jackson, MA All Rights Reserved
Graphic Artist: JACKIE HERNANDEZ

Which character traits would be most useful to you right now and why?

Draw or write about it here.

How to Use the "Victim Mode vs. Warrior Mode" Poster to Feel Happier and More Free

This poster is designed to help you recognize and shift the types of questions you ask yourself so you can feel more empowered, happier, and free—no matter what's going on around you. It's all about taking control of your thoughts.

Understanding the Two Modes:

- **Victim Mode**: When you're stuck in Victim Mode, your thoughts are typically negative, and they often come in the form of automatic questions like, "Why me?" or "Why is life unfair?" These types of questions make you feel worse because they focus on what's wrong and make you feel powerless.
- **Warrior Mode**: On the other hand, Warrior Mode questions are about finding solutions, staying strong, and focusing on what you can control. Questions like "How can I make the best of this?" or "What can I do right now to feel better?" will make you feel more positive and empowered.

How to Use the Poster:

1. **Check in with Yourself**: When you feel down or upset, take a moment to notice what you're thinking. Are you asking Victim Mode questions like "Why is this happening to me?" If so, that's why you're feeling worse.
2. **Flip the Script**: Look at the Warrior Mode questions on the poster. For example, if you're thinking, "It's not fair," flip it to, "How can I turn this around for my good?" Just asking a different question can shift your mood and perspective.
3. **Take Back Control**: Remember, even when things feel out of your control, you still have power over your thoughts. The subconscious mind tends to make us feel like we've lost control over everything when one thing goes wrong. But that's not true! Focus on what you *can* control—your interpretation of the situation and your response.
4. **Make It a Habit**: The more you practice shifting from Victim Mode to Warrior Mode, the easier it becomes to feel better and take control of your emotions. Use the poster as a reminder to keep practicing this skill.

The Key to Feeling Happier and Free

At any moment, you have the power to choose your thoughts. If you catch yourself feeling bad, it's a signal that you're thinking in Victim Mode. The secret to happiness and freedom lies in choosing to think Warrior Mode thoughts. By focusing on what you *can* do and asking empowering questions, you'll feel stronger, more positive, and in control of your life.

Feel free to refer to this poster whenever you need a reminder!

HOW TO FEEL BETTER!

VICTIM MODE   WARRIOR MODE

Victim Mode	Warrior Mode
 • Why me???	• What can I do to make myself feel better now, that's good for me? 
 • How come I can't get what I want?	• How can I make the best of this? 
 • Why didn't they have to!?	• How can I prevent people from making me feel bad? 
 • It's not fair!!	• How can I turn this out for my good? 

RESILIENCE MEANS:

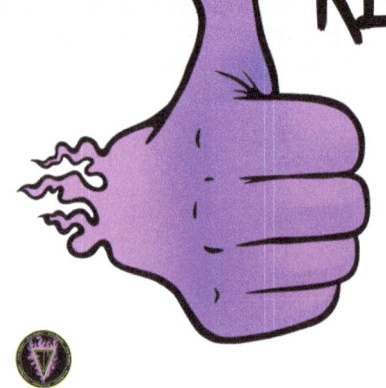

WHATEVER HAPPENS I CAN HANDLE IT!